The Revolution and Independence of the FreeWorld

- The early self-government
- Land Policy
- Rights in the colony
- The bid for independence
- Colonial resistance
- The decision for independence
- The Treaty of Paris

Pedro M. Anderson

The Revolution

and

Independence

of

the FreeWorld

Pedro M. Anderson

Copyright

All rights reserved. No part of this publication should be reprinted or transmitted through electronic or mechanical means without prior permission by the Author, except for citations for critical uses.

DEDICATION

This work is dedicated to the Almighty God for helping me throughout writing this book and also this work is dedicated to the entire people of our great nation most especially our Fathers who fought through blood and sweat to see the independence of America.

ACKNOWLEDGMENTS

Throughout the entire process of writing this book, my parents; Fidelis and Perpetua, also my big Aunty; Felicia have all been supportive and made sure that all I needed to make this a reality were available. I also want to appreciate my mentor Abraham Aiyejinna and also my wonderful friends; Bruno and Collins who have been there during my challenging times in this work. May the Lord bless you all.

Table of Contents

Prologue
Brief History of Independence Day
Early self-government and colonization
How colonization took place
Self-initial government's steps
Land policy in New England and Virginia
Founding of the middle colonies
The Carolinas and Georgia
New shapes of colonial development
Imperial organization
Rights in the colonies
The contest with France
Competing claims in North America
The French and Indian War
American social and cultural development
The bid for independence (1763–83)
Earlier disagreements
New colonial policy
Proclamation line
Trade with Native Americans
Regulation of maritime trade
Grenville taxes of 1764
The Stamp Act
The Quartering Act
Conflicting views of the new policy
The Stamp Act crisis
Repeal of the Stamp Act
The tasks of Townshend
Colonial resistance
The Boston Massacre

The Gaspee
The colonies join hands
The Boston Tea Party
The Intolerable Acts
Revolution and independence
The First Continental Congress
Parliament's response
The decision for independence
Howe's peace mission
The turning point
War in the south
Yorktown
The Treaty of Paris

Prologue

The Fourth of July, often known as Independence Day or July 4th, has been a federal holiday in the US since 1941, but Independence Day celebrations have a long history dating back to the American Revolution in the 18th century. The Declaration of Independence, a significant document written by Thomas Jefferson, was adopted by representatives from the 13 colonies two days after the Continental Congress voted in favor of independence on July 2, 1776. Since 1776, July 4th has been observed as the beginning of American freedom, and celebrations have included everything from fireworks, parades, and concerts to more laid-back family get-togethers and barbecues. Monday, July 4, 2022, marks the Fourth of July.

Brief History of Independence Day

Few colonists, including those who were radicals, wanted complete independence from Great Britain as the Revolutionary War's first battles broke out in April 1775.

However, by the middle of the following year, more colonists were in favor of independence due to growing antipathy against Britain and the dissemination of revolutionary ideas, such as those outlined in Thomas Paine's best-selling pamphlet "Common Sense," which was released in the early 1776.

Richard Henry Lee, a delegate from Virginia, proposed a motion calling for the colonies' independence when the Continental Congress convened at the Pennsylvania State House (later Independence Hall) in Philadelphia on June 7.

The vote on Lee's resolution was postponed by Congress after a contentious debate, but Thomas Jefferson of Virginia, John Adams of Massachusetts, Roger Sherman of Connecticut, Benjamin Franklin of Pennsylvania, and Robert R. Livingston of New York were named to a five-person committee to draft a formal justification for the break with Great Britain.

Did you also know? John Adams reportedly turned down invitations to attend at July 4th gatherings in protest because he thought that July 2nd should be the appropriate day to commemorate the beginning of American independence. On July 4, 1826—the 50th anniversary of the Declaration of Independence's adoption—Adams and Thomas Jefferson both passed away.

The Continental Congress approved Lee's resolution for independence on July 2nd with a nearly unanimous vote (the New York delegation abstained, but later voted affirmatively). John Adams informed his wife Abigail in a letter that day that July 2 "would be remembered, by future Generations, as the grand anniversary Festival" and that the event should feature "Pomp and Parade...Games, Sports, Guns, Bells, Bonfires and Illuminations from one End of this Continent."

Early self-government and colonization

The majority of people living in the colonies in the 17th century were of English descent, with Africans making up the second-largest group. During the 18th century, a lot of German and Scotch-Irish immigrants came. The Netherlands, Scotland, and France all made significant ethnic contributions to the colonial ethnic mix. Except for Pennsylvania, where there were more English than German settlers, New England was almost entirely made up of English settlers. In the southern colonies, the English made up the majority of the settlers of European descent. The English language and culture were dominant throughout, except for little Dutch and German pockets that gradually disappeared.

During the colonial era, the "melting pot" started to boil, and Gov. William Livingston, who was three-fourths Dutch and one-fourth Scottish, identified as an Anglo-Saxon. While all of them tended to diverge from the residents of "the old land," they all became more like the English when the other aspects blended with them. On both sides of the Atlantic by 1763, the term "American" was frequently employed to describe the inhabitants of the 13 colonies.

Three nations—France, Spain, and England—were vying for dominance in North America at the beginning of the 17th century. Of these, England was the last to arrive on the scene and was ultimately in charge of the early stages of the United States. The French, who were burdened by internal religious strife and external conflicts, were slow to grasp the tremendous potential of the new continent, and their settlements in the St. Lawrence Valley grew slowly.

The regions surrounded by the Caribbean Sea and the Gulf of Mexico were of particular interest to the Spaniards, as were South America. But after initial failures under Sir Humphrey Gilbert and Sir Walter Raleigh, the English established strong settlements from Maine to Georgia, fed them with a steady flow of people and money, and quickly absorbed the smaller colonizing endeavours of the Dutch in the Hudson Valley and the tiny Swedish effort on the Delaware River. Massachusetts, New Hampshire, Rhode Island, Connecticut, New York, Pennsylvania, Delaware, New Jersey, Maryland, Virginia, North Carolina, South Carolina, and Georgia were among the 13 prosperous colonies the British had established on the Atlantic coast within a century and a half.

The colonists quickly moved from the Tidewater region toward the Appalachians before finally navigating the Cumberland Gap and Ohio River to cross the mountains. They changed from being more European in habit and viewpoint to being more American decade after decade, with the frontier particularly leaving its mark. They were quite individualistic since they were free from the majority of the feudal legacies of western Europe and had to develop self-reliance to control nature.

How colonization took place

Political, religious, and economic factors all had a role in the settlement of the Atlantic coast. By 1600, both labour and capital in England had become quite mobile and were looking for more lucrative industries. Many people became restless as prices and living expenses skyrocketed; others were driven from the land by increased sheep grazing and the fencing of once-common lands; and brave young men, including younger sons of the gentry, lost the occupation that the wars with Spain had given them, looked abroad. Many Englishmen believed that Spain, Portugal, and other nations should compete because they believed that the colonization of the New World may increase the might and prosperity of their own country.
Finally, the spread of great commercial trading companies assisted in the work.

The crown granted charters to these businesses to expand England's international markets. For instance, the Levant Company oversaw trade with Venice and the Near East, while the East India Company (1600) protected the coasts of the Pacific and Indian Oceans. The Muscovy Company, founded in 1555, had as its goal trading with Russia. Additionally, companies were set up for Bermuda, the Northwest Passage, and Newfoundland. The two corporations that King James I awarded charters to in 1606—one to populate the American coast anywhere between parallels 34° and 41° north and the other anywhere between 38° and 45° north—were the most significant for America.

The first firm was known as the Virginia Company of London (Virginia Company) because its members resided in London, while the second was known as the Plymouth Company because its members lived in Plymouth. Investors in the firms were expected to provide the companies with capital and settlers, and to manage trade and production. However, the monarch was to continue to have control over the government by using councils. Without specifying their exact parameters, all of the liberties and rights enjoyed by English subjects were guaranteed to the colonists. In exchange, the grantees were prohibited from drafting any commands or regulations that conflicted with those of England.

Quick to exercise its authority, the Virginia Company. Before Christmas in 1606, three ships sailed for Virginia, carrying among others Bartholomew Gosnold, a former visitor to the New England coast, and Capt. John Smith, who would play a significant role in the history of the United States. The three ships arrived in Hampton Roads in the spring of 1607, christened the James River, landed 120 men, and established Jamestown. Despite the arrival of additional ships carrying new people, the colony had a period of uncertain existence due to starvation, disease, and Indian warfare. In the end, Virginia established a strong foundation: "We aspire to construct a nation / Where none before has stood," one of the early explorers sang in a ballad, and they succeeded in their goal.

The Virginia Company had expanded its legal standing during these years. In 1609 and 1612, the crown granted it two brand-new charters. These additional awards reaffirmed to it a vast belt of territory that was 400 miles (640 km) broad and stretched over the American continent to the Pacific Ocean, thus severing it from the Plymouth Company. Thus, ownership of the Virginian colony passed to the Virginia Company. It also acquired significant government rights during the same period. It had complete authority over the resident governor, his resident council, and all other officers. Private property in land and stores replaced the previous joint-stock system of managing trade and real estate. With three ships, 300 colonists, and some animals, an accomplished soldier named Sir Thomas Dale arrived in Virginia in 1611 and exercised statesmanlike leadership for five years. The colony successfully started growing tobacco during these years.

Near the same time, the Plymouth Company's attempt to establish a colony at the Maine river's mouth had failed. What is now New England was not further colonized until a group of Separatists, who held that the Bible was the only source of faith and rebelled against all other religions, shifted their attention to this region. These Pilgrims joined forces with a group of traders and other businesses who agreed to provide funding for the project.

The colonists agreed to work for seven years and put all of their earnings into a communal pot in exchange for quick cash advances; during that time, both profits and land were to remain undivided. One of the two ships sent back was the Mayflower, but the other left on September 16 (New Style; September 6 Old Style) in 1620 with roughly 100 people and arrived in Cape Cod before the year was through. The colony at Plymouth, Massachusetts, established itself after great suffering and danger were bravely faced. Within ten years it was expanding prosperously, had cut links with its English partners, and had abandoned the joint-stock structure in favour of private assets and business ventures.

Self-initial government's steps

The colonists soon started to exert some autonomy in both Virginia and New England. A significant stride forward was made in 1619 when Governor George Yeardley presented a new governance structure to Jamestown. A two-part legislature was established, with the governor and his council—named by the company in England—making up one half, and a house composed of two burgesses from each settlement—making up the other. Subject to the governor's and the company's approval, it was to pass laws governing domestic matters in Virginia.

In Jamestown's log chapel, the first authentic continental American legislature convened throughout the summer. Later, just before boarding their ship, the Pilgrims ratified the Mayflower Compact. It was an understanding that they would coexist in peace with city officials of their choosing rather than a type of governance. John Carver was chosen as governor on board the ship; William Bradford would take over soon after. The Plymouth colonists convened the first New England town meeting as soon as they started building their own homes and conferred on the laws that would govern both their civil and military governments.

Nevertheless, a colony of stronger individuality and more assertive self-governance was about to be founded. The "Great Migration" of Puritans from England to America took place between 1630 and 1642. These people were unhappy with King Charles I, who in 1629 disbanded Parliament for 11 years, and with Archbishop William Laud, who declared war on them. They believed in a church free of outdated practices and abuses and a society free of heinous vices. John Winthrop, a country squire with tremendous vitality, and John Endecott, who guided a group of settlers to Salem, Massachusetts, demonstrated exceptional leadership. The Massachusetts Bay Company received a charter from the crown in 1629.

It was swiftly taken over by the Puritans, and Winthrop, who was governor, persuaded the members to decide in favour of sending the company, the charter, and a sizable group of colonists to Boston, Massachusetts. This Massachusetts Bay colony, with Boston as its capital, had an immediate influx of new tribes. According to careful calculations, 20,000 people had arrived in America by 1641 on 300 ships. There were a few nobles and a large number of university graduates in this virtually entirely English exodus. Most of the migrants were driven by religious devotion.

As a result, a church state was established that was far from democratic but cherished freedom and self-rule. Every town in Massachusetts Bay was a separate Congregational community with its church, pastor, and town government. Church members only could vote, and the clergy held significant civic authority. In the general court, or legislature, where they, the governor, and a small group of his deputies made laws and imposed taxes, the voting freemen began electing deputies as early as possible. A self-sufficient, oligarchical commonwealth was born as a result. It was proclaimed to have unfettered self-government under the crown and to owe neither allegiance nor reverence to the English Parliament by Governor Winthrop and others. However, the domination of the clergy and the rigidity and stifling nature of their governance stoked a great deal of unrest.

The yearning for more independence in politics and religion, along with the restlessness of individuals seeking better land, propelled some New Englanders to find other colonies. Thus, the Rev. John Davenport and others built the New Haven colony, which later spread along Long Island Sound, Thomas Hooker and others founded settlements on the Connecticut River, and Roger Williams, a fervent supporter of freedom and tolerance, contributed to the creation of Rhode Island. Massachusetts Bay ruled the early residents of Maine and New Hampshire. Up until 1680, every New Englander ran his affairs. While passing their, conducting business according to their own rules, and building their armed forces for defence, they still viewed the English government as sovereign. Their relationship with England was one of sentiment, not of need, and they were free to pursue their interests.

The colonies benefited from the home country's preoccupation with its affairs, particularly during the Civil War and Commonwealth in England. The Massachusetts legislature made the audacious claim that New England was not subject to English Parliament regulations. Virginia was allowed to choose its rnor, council, and burgesses under Oliver Cromwell and the Commonwealth. The New England Confederation, which lasted for a whole generation, was created in 1643 by the four colonies of Massachusetts Bay, Plymouth, Connecticut, and New Haven during a time of civil unrest in England. Its main objective was to defeat nice against the French, the Dutch, and the Native Americans, but it also dealt with boundary disputes and offered "mutual advise" on a variety of issues.

Land policy in New England and Virginia

Group settlement was the method used to expand the New England colonies. A migratory group would get a land grant from the general courts of the various colonies, most notably Massachusetts Bay, with meticulously drawn boundaries. Then, this group would find a new town. The general court or legislature governed its common lands, fencing, grazing techniques, and method of allocating farms, but each town then assumed jurisdiction over land allotments and maintenance. Who would be allowed to become settlers and freeholders in the town was decided by the legislature. The land of each community was first divided into house lots, common fields, meadows, and pastures by the town meetings or boards of town proprietors. Each town's residents typically lived near one another for safety and socialization while travelling from the town centre to work their land. With no lord of the manor in charge, the average town was therefore quite similar to an English manor. Of course, the town served as the location of the church, and the pastor served as the mayor. The town served as the focal point for taxation, elections, and militia duty.

Settlement in Virginia happened in a very different way. The colonists quickly moved westward as far as the James River Falls, where Richmond is now located, after dispersing widely along the creeks and rivers. They farmed land in far bigger units known as plantations, with almost no community centres, and they utilized servants—and, importantly, slaves—much more than New England did, in part because tobacco quickly depleted the soil. This pattern was unfavourable for interpersonal relationships, teamwork, and communal endeavours, but it fostered an independent spirit on par with that seen further north. The planters favoured white indentured workers over African slaves throughout the 17th century, and for a period as many as 1,500 came each year. They were mostly English, with a small number of Scots and Irish, and they typically agreed to work without pay for four to six years in exchange for transportation and support. This redemptioner or indenture system became a very effective tool for colonization. The servants proceeded up the streams, acquired land, started transporting tobacco from their wharves, and then transformed into independent planters or freehold farmers once their terms had been agreed upon.

Parishes and counties were Virginia's basic political subdivisions. In the English system, parish institutions were primarily ecclesiastical but also included education; each minister ran a school and the vestry made sure that all underprivileged children could read and write. Private tutors were typically available to wealthy families' children. To keep up with the increasing population growth, the counties expanded in size. Virginia had 13 counties by 1652, with 2 on the York River and 9 on the James River. The county courts frequently fell under the influence of a small number of powerful families and held significant local government authority. The House of Burgesses was essentially elected by manhood suffrage up until 1636; after that, the vote was curtailed, and Sir William Berkeley, the Restoration's governor, maintained a compliant house in office for 15 years.

Founding of the middle colonies

The goal of Henry Hudson's 1609 journey to what is now New York Bay was to trade. Trades to co shipments were sought by the Dutch. However, the Dutch West India Company was granted authority by the Dutch government to build forts, form governments, and conquer large swaths of land, including the American coast, in 1621. A vessel carrying 30 Walloon families, Protestant exiles from the southern provinces of the Netherlands, was transported by the company's leaders two years later to the mouth of the Hudson River, where they established the first permanent settlement on the island of Manhattan. The number of settlers increased, and in 1626 Peter Minuit "bought" the island from Indian sachems (who historians have variously identified as belonging to the Lenape, Delaware, Munsee, or Algonquin people) and established New Amsterdam as the colony's capital. As a fur trading post, Fort Orange (now Albany) had been established up the Hudson two years earlier. New Amsterdam swiftly attracted individuals from other countries and religions, developing into a multicultural city. It was filled with privateers, smugglers, tavern owners, and rowdy sailors and had the independent, anarchic feel of a seaport.

New Netherland did not expand as quickly as the English colonies for a variety of reasons. In the beginning, the Dutch West India Company was much more interested in exploiting Spanish trade in the Caribbean and Atlantic than in locating long-term residents. Additionally, it wanted to expand the fur trade and participate in the tobacco industry. When it started to seriously consider settlement, it used a poor strategy. Starting in 1629, it offered each patroon who brought out 50 families a large estate to settle them on as tenants, with the owner retaining certain monopolies, such as milling. A few powerful families obtained an unhealthy amount of riches and power under this type of feudalism. There were a few sparsely distributed independent farms or boweries started by local small farmers as well as a few stray New England Puritans who settled in Westchester and the northern parts of Long Island. Last but not least, the Dutch West India Company's appointed governors and councils were harsh, authoritarian, and inept since they lacked the kind of public assemblies that Virginia and New England did. They did not become particularly well-liked and were frequently despised. Peter Stuyvesant, the most well-known governor, was also the most brazen and obtuse.

It was unthinkable for England to allow a Dutch colony to sever its territories along the Atlantic coast for an extended period. Without firing a shot, a small English naval force in 1664 forced the New Netherlands to submit. The 7,000 locals accepted the new government without opposition. The colony of New York, which stretched from the Connecticut River to Delaware, was given to Charles II's brother James, the Duke of York, to manage and own. A more liberal regime started right away. The landowner dispatched a governor with orders to treat the local Dutch people well, let them maintain their lands, and avoid interfering with their language or religion. Settlements grew denser and immigration was promoted. A representative assembly for the province of New York was called by Governor Thomas Dongan in 1683.

The creation of what would become Pennsylvania and Delaware was overseen by one of the greatest of all colonial leaders. William Penn, the well-known English admiral Sir William Penn's son, joined the Society of Friends, also known as the Quakers, in his early 20s in 1667. He desired to build a colony where every religious group could live in freedom on both a political and religious level. William Penn was able to seize control of a sizable portion of the imperial estate given to the duke of York thanks to his friendship with the Duke of York and the fact that the king owed Admiral Penn a sizable outstanding debt. He started seeking immigrants as soon as the crown granted him a private charter in 1681. He published a four-language guide to Pennsylvania and generously offered people land: 50 acres for free, larger farms for a little nominal cost, and 5,000 acres for £100. In 1682, Penn paid a visit to his "holy experiment." And in that same year, he established a constitution that called for a smaller elected council to meet with him as governor and propose laws, as well as a bigger elective assembly to approve or reject them. The assembly soon acquired considerably greater authority and began to propose its legislation. A new charter was issued by Penn in 1701, and it stood until the American Revolution.

It is not surprising that Pennsylvania outperformed other colonies in terms of growth. Large numbers of immigrants, mainly from England and Germany, went there to take advantage of the country's potential for trade and manufacturing as well as its religious freedom and humane criminal laws. Philadelphia, Penn's "city of brotherly love," was both a beautiful and a prosperous city. Penn had hoped that it would always be "a green country town," with gardens surrounding every house. The colony had a unique atmosphere because of Quakerism, which had softened from its initially relatively rigorous outlines. Many of the institutions on which America later took great pride were put to the test in Pennsylvania, including complete religious liberty, the affordable distribution of land to actual settlers, the promotion of racial diversity, and the development of top-notch public schools. The Quakers' high moral and intellectual standards soon led to a remarkable elevation of Pennsylvania's cultural level. It was renowned for its elegant mansions, libraries, scientific curiosity, and taste in architecture. It established the first printing press outside of New England while it was only ten years old.

Before his passing, Penn acquired three counties along the Delaware River from the Duke of York, which later gave rise to the province and state of the same name. Despite having a common governor with Pennsylvania, they started having their own elected assembly in 1702. Beginning with proprietors, so did the other middle colonies. Due to its early role as a haven for Roman Catholics, Maryland has a unique history that is worth exploring. George Calvert, 1st Baron Baltimore, who was keenly interested in colonization, was given the region between the Potomac River and the 40th parallel by Charles I in 1632. His son, Cecilius Calvert, 2nd Baron Baltimore, assumed control of the gift almost immediately and decided to found a colony where his fellow Roman Catholics might live in harmony. Early in 1634, a shipload of Roman Catholic settlers picked St. Marys, a location on a Potomac tributary close to its mouth. Since Roman Catholics decided to remain in England, Protestants soon made up the bulk of the settlers. Cecilius Calvert convinced the assembly he convened in 1649 to pass an act of religious tolerance in response to this circumstance. Unfortunately, this law was quickly revoked.

Maryland had a difficult past while benefiting from Virginia's proximity, which provided it with trade and protection. The gifts of property, positions, and favours that Calvert gave to his family and Roman Catholic cronies infuriated the Protestant settlers. Additionally, they found it irritating how little power he gave his assembly. Conflict over theological and economic issues reached its height in 1654 when the Protestant small farmers finally achieved their major goals. The Calvert family lost possession of Maryland when William and Mary took the throne in England in 1689; however, the family reclaimed its rights in 1715 after a new Lord Baltimore converted to Protestantism.

In the interim, the name and jurisdiction of the future state of New Jersey had undergone some confusing and unsuccessful modifications. The territory that is now known as New Jersey was originally given to two friends, Lord John Berkeley and Sir George Carteret, by the duke of York, the original owner, as the province of Nova Cesaria. They created a charter or collection of "concessions and agreements" to entice new settlers, which broadly predicted Penn's liberal ideologies. They provided total freedom of conscience, a popular assembly, and favourable terms for purchasing land. Berkeley sold his portion to two Quakers in 1674, who then acquired the southwest corner of what would become the state. The northeastern half was sold by Carteret's widow to new landowners in 1680. In the end, both parts were seized by the crown in 1702.

The Carolinas and Georgia

Under royal concessions to powerful owners, the territories south of Virginia were also inhabited. Eight persons gained a gift of all of North America between the 31st and 36th parallels during the reign of Charles II. This wonderful domain's two components were created in quite distinct methods. Charleston, South Carolina, was established in 1670 by Sir John Colleton and Anthony Ashley Cooper, afterwards known as Lord Shaftesbury, together with immigrants from Barbados and England.

By the year 1700, South Carolina had roughly 5,000 people living there, including black slaves, thanks to waves of immigration from French Huguenots and Scots. The colony's early economy depended on exporting grain to the West Indies as well as turpentine, tar, and furs to Europe. Following the introduction of rice from Madagascar, South Carolinians established sizable estates where they successfully farmed both rice and indigo. While this was happening, a variety of immigrants—including English, Germans, drifters from Virginia, and intrepid New Englanders—settled the region to the north on moderate-sized farms. One particularly wealthy component was a Swiss community in New Bern.

The "Fundamental Constitutions," drafted by John Locke with Shaftesbury's assistance for the Carolinas and establishing a hereditary landed nobility with absurd titles, were completely inappropriate for the American context and were never put into practice. Instead, the owners provided each colony with a straightforward, functional system of government that included a governor, council, and assembly. Similar to Virginia, the Carolinas had a very dispersed population. While other towns were few and small, Charleston developed into a luxurious and chic small city. The two colonies were very different in terms of social and economic nature. When compared to South Carolina's staples, North Carolina discovered that its tobacco and naval stores, supplied from shoddy ports, offered significantly less revenue. It had very few outstanding planters and lacked the merchants and ship captains Charleston had. Only a few coastal settlements could boast of the aristocratic environment that was developing in the southern colonies, and its population tended to be poorer and less educated. Many planters in South Carolina amassed riches at their country estates, where they spent the majority of the year. They lived in elegant townhouses in Charleston, where they maintained a delightful social life with wealthy businessmen and a strong professional class during the sweltering summer months. They gave the assembly, also known as the commons house, an English accent. However, North Carolina's white population increased more quickly, and its slave population was lower than that of its southern neighbour.

A group of British philanthropists formed Georgia, the latest of the 13 colonies to be established. These landowners planned to provide creditors and other deserving poor people with a fresh start by getting a grant of property between the Savannah and Altamaha rivers. Gen. James Oglethorpe and 100 settlers were sent there in 1733 to find the town of Savannah. The trustees established some rules that were more idealistic than practical. To prevent the development of large estates, every charity colonist was limited to 50 acres (20 hectares) of land, which he could only pass on to a male heir. Slavery was also prohibited. Georgia's development was slowed by this benevolent paternalism. The early settlers soon realized that greater plots of land were necessary for profitable tillage and that using slave labour would be beneficial. They desired to trade their logs for imports of West Indian rum. The trustees progressively relaxed their regulations, allowing the colonists to choose an assembly in 1751. When their proprietorship's term expired the following year, they did not attempt to renew it and instead let the crown seize control of Georgia.

It was still so feeble as a royal colony and required ongoing support. It formed a society of slave-owning landowners in the lowlands, merchants in Savannah, and small farmers in the uplands, and its agriculture resembled South Carolina's more and more. However, the philanthropists had produced three worthwhile outcomes: they had saved a sizable number of victims of neglect and abuse; they had preserved a barrier between the other southern colonies and Spanish Florida, and they had established the groundwork for one of the most powerful southern states.

New shapes of colonial development

Three major new forces started to transform the British colonies in North America in the 80 years between 1660 and 1740. They were the trade and navigation laws that governed the economy, the incomplete organization of imperial government, and the struggle with the French for control of the continent. The colonists were probably about 250,000 strong by the year 1700, and they were expanding at a rate that has rarely been matched in the history of Western nations. This expansion was accelerated by immigration, early marriage, the economic worth of children in an agricultural society, and generally good health.

English economic policy viewed the colonies as a component of an imperial total that should strive for self-sufficiency and a favourable trade balance under the concept of mercantilism broadly embraced by western Europe. Each region of the empire had resources to provide and benefits to receive. Three Navigation Acts passed by Parliament in 1651, 1660, and 1663 were the first to include this policy. According to the rule of 1651, any products imported into England or its colonies had to be transported aboard ships with English owners, captains, and crew (colonials, of course, were considered Englishmen). All products imported into England and the colonies from Europe were exempt from this regulation since they might arrive in ships from the nation that produced the items.

The 1660 statute strengthened the original by mandating that ships used to transport products into and out of England be built, owned, and staffed in England or the colonies. Additionally, it stipulated that some "enumerated products," primarily sugar, tobacco, and indigo, may only be exported to England or other British possessions. No one was allowed to grow tobacco in England or import it from another country to give the colonists complete control over the domestic market. The 1663 law was more severe. It required that European commodities be sent to the colonies via England, which required many colonial merchants to extend their journeys by an additional leg.

Many colonists tried to avoid committing these crimes. They imported products directly from Europe without stopping at English ports, and they delivered the specified items to Europe rather than to England. Then, Parliament passed new legislation in 1673 and 1696 to put an end to the evasions. Additionally, the list of specified items was expanded, resulting in the control of essential commodities for the colonies including copper, furs, rice, molasses, and naval provisions (tar, pitch, and turpentine) by the year 1721. The Molasses Act, which imposed severe taxes on all sugar, molasses, rum, and other spirits imported into the colonies from the French, Dutch, and Spanish domains, was passed by the British Parliament in 1733. The intention was to impose trade restrictions on the British West Indies. This law would have been terrible if it had been put into effect because the colonies traded massive amounts of fish, lumber, meat, and food with the foreign islands in exchange for these commodities. Thankfully, the British authorities ignored the widespread infractions.

To protect the colonial market for its industries, the mother nation placed other bothersome restrictions on the colonies' ability to create goods. The export of woollen fabrics beyond any colonial border was outlawed by the Wool Act of 1699. Similar restrictions, including a cap on the number of apprentices, were imposed by the Hat Act of 1732. The Iron Act of 1750 prevented the construction of rolling and slitting mills, forges, and iron-making facilities in the colonies toward the end of the colonial era. The British government anticipated inflation that would harm British creditors and increase the cost of colonial exports because, like all new societies, the colonies required a more plentiful currency than they did and desired to issue paper money. As a result, they prohibited New England from issuing paper money in 1751, and they extended the prohibition to the other colonies in 1764.

The mercantilist laws, however, were far from punitive overall and contained numerous aspects that were advantageous to the colonies. The laws governing navigation encouraged shipbuilding in the colonies. The British market was handed to some significant American items as a monopoly. Colonial pig iron and bar iron were allowed duty-free entry into Great Britain. On the creation of naval supplies, Britain paid bounties. These factors, along with Robert Walpole's benevolent neglect of the colonies and the lack of execution of the harsher rules, allowed for the steady growth of American commercial activity. The British army and navy were still able to defend the colonists. However, two facts about the trade legislation had an impact on subsequent events. The colonies were used as a market for manufactured goods as well as a supply of cheap raw resources by the elder countries, and they resented this treatment just like other frontier agricultural communities did. Second, a culture of disobedience and insubordination was established among the colonists as a result of widespread law-breaking.

Imperial organization

The list of royal provinces grew longer over time. The proprietary colony of New York assumed the new status upon the succession of the Duke of York to the throne and remained there. In 1679, New Hampshire was proclaimed a royal province. The extensive free autonomy of Massachusetts Bay came to an abrupt end with the return of the Stuarts. Charges that the Puritans had broken their charter and disobeyed imperial decrees were investigated by a royal commission. Charles II abrogated the charter and instituted special colonial governance procedures in 1684 as a result of ongoing unrest. Massachusetts was the first state to have a single governor, along with Maine, New Hampshire, and a portion of Rhode Island. Then, in 1686, Sir Edmund Andros arrived with orders to establish the Dominion of New England over the entirety of New England, New York, and New Jersey. The Glorious Revolution of 1688–1689 in England put an end to his oppressive rule, nonetheless, and Massachusetts Bay skillfully negotiated a new charter with William and Mary that included Plymouth in the colony.

Eight of the colonies had become royal provinces by the reign of George I. Under their original charters, Connecticut and Rhode Island were practically small republics; Pennsylvania and Maryland continued to be governed by proprietary systems, and Georgia struggled under its trustees until 1752. Some British politicians wanted to see all the colonies placed under unified royal rule, but succeeding ministries resisted, not wanting to incite popular unrest or strengthen the crown's position. All colonies had representative assemblies that oversaw budgets, filled several positions, and were frequently in direct conflict with the royal governors or proprietors. Rhode Island and Connecticut both have independent governor elections. In these ongoing disputes, the colonists fared best because they acted more skillfully and persistently out of self-interest. Representative self-government, however, was not the same as a genuine democracy. Because all of the colonies were granted voting rights based on property, the poorest citizens were not represented in the assembly. Additionally, the older seaboard communities made sure that their communities received more seats than the newer frontier settlements.

The parliament made an effort to curtail the executive's authority in every royal and proprietary colony. They gradually reduced the power of the governor and increased the power of the legislature by using their ability to tax as a lever. They oversaw the fees that the executive relied on, converted appointive roles into elective ones, and often staged uprisings against governors' councils and other "official cliques." Thus, the popular government expanded decade after decade. After 1701, all legislation was controlled by the assembly in one province, Pennsylvania, which had no legislative council.

The crown, operating through the secretary of state and Privy Council, held ultimate power over English America. However, it was assigned to a series of boards or committees: first, in 1660, to the Privy Council committee for foreign plantations; second, in 1675, to the Privy Council committee known as the lords of trade; and third, in 1696, to the commissioners of trade and plantations, which were independent of the Privy Council. However, maintaining tight control was impractical; it was dispersed throughout several organizations. The treasury board monitored expenditures for the colonies, audited colonial revenue, and carefully considered appointments to the colonial service. The outfitting of the navy on American seas, the protection of commerce, and the punishment of smugglers were all topics covered by the admiralty board. The military affairs in the colonies were under the jurisdiction of the war office. The bishop of London oversaw the hiring of Anglican pastors and kept an eye on their behaviour and the parish schools they helped maintain. The Privy Council handled colonial business by receiving letters and petitions, setting up hearings and enquiries, and issuing letters, directives, and orders in council on a wide range of topics. The court served as a colonial court of appeals as well.

As a result, the administration needed a sizable bureaucracy. But over time, a significant amount of business was handled directly by one of the secretaries of state's office in London, bypassing the Privy Council. In other words, the cabinet assumed control, with the secretary of state for the southern department playing a particularly significant role. Many colonies despatched spies to London, like Benjamin Franklin, or recruited competent British citizens, like Edmund Burke, to ensure that their viewpoints were adequately communicated. Imperial governance was typically lax rather than severe. This was made possible by the colonies' extreme isolation; it took at least three months to reply to a letter sent from England to New York. The crown authorities were complacent due to a combination of factors including distance, a tradition of leaving well enough alone, and the conviction that Americans could competently handle their affairs. The colonists had more political freedom before 1760 than maybe any other people on the planet. They had access to numerous rights and advantages that were completely unheard of in French and Spanish territories.

Rights in the colonies

Up until 1760, Parliament only passed a total of roughly 100laws laws about colonies, the majority of which dealt with political and economic issues. The English fundamental rights protections were highly valued by all of the provinces, some of which adopted significant portions of the English statute law. All of British America automatically adopted the English common law. Although the king in council normally compelled the colonial assemblies after 1690 to send their acts to England for approval or disapproval, this was not a significant burden. The expansion of colonial territory, setting of boundaries, and preservation of commercial interests were the imperial government's key concerns as the 18th century went on. The Anglican (Episcopal) church and its finances received significant attention as well.

By the conclusion of the colonial era, Connecticut, Massachusetts, and New Hampshire had established Puritan or Congregational churches. The Anglican church expanded itself further south in the Carolinas, Georgia, Virginia, and Maryland, as well as in four southern counties of New York, but its hold in North Carolina and western Virginia was tenuous. Church and state were kept distinct in the other colonies of Rhode Island, Pennsylvania, Delaware, and New Jersey. Religious tolerance was unaffected by the discrimination present in Congregational and Episcopal institutions.

Contrarily, compared to most other parts of the world in the 18th century, British America was much more tolerant of religious freedom drawing settlers, the crown, various landowners, and significant colonial interests encouraged a variety of religious sects: Jews to New York and Rhode Island, Huguenots to South Carolina and New York, Mennonites, Dunkards, and other German sects to Pennsylvania, Scotch-Irish Presbyterians to lands as far away as North Carolina, and Roman Catholics to Maryland. This range of denominations contributed to the freedom of religion. Although Jews were a minority in several colonies, they were prohibited from holding office and from voting. Roman Catholics in most colonies experienced considerable limitations (partially brought on by a fear of the French), but they also had significantly greater freedom than Protestants in Roman Catholic countries.

The spirit of colonial life was supportive of intellectual freedom in all disciplines. As the 18th century progressed, the established churches' hold over both New England and the southern provinces steadily eroded. In addition to Deism among academics, dissenting sects flourished quickly among the general populace. Taxation for the construction of churches inevitably led to growing anger. The Great Awakening, a religious revival that peaked in the 1730s, may have been a sign that the older churches had failed to give the populace the emotional and intellectual nourishment they need. It was led in Massachusetts by Jonathan Edwards, a persuasive Yale alumnus whose sermons dealt with faith, sin, and punishment; in the middle colonies by William Tennent, a zealous preacher who came from Scotland and established a "log college" in Pennsylvania for training other zealous clergymen; and in Georgia by the unflappable George Whitefield, who soon began touring other colonies and mesmerized enormous crowds everywhere. The movement persisted vigorously throughout the 1740s, won over large numbers of people, and, by fostering a spirit of rebellion against traditional religious practices, gave the Baptists, the Presbyterians, and eventually the John Wesley-led Methodists fresh life.

The colonists enjoyed at least equal rights to free speech, assembly, and the press to those enjoyed by the British at home. John Peter Zenger was detained for libel after he let a prominent New York politician criticize the royal governor in his New York Weekly Journal. The elderly but tenacious Andrew Hamilton, a Philadelphia lawyer, successfully secured Zenger's freedom with a passionate appeal to the jury by arguing that basic British liberty was at risk. America soon became a land of newspapers, as evidenced by this case. Except for Delaware and New Jersey, every colony had at least one by 1765, when the total was 25. Even fewer inhibitions than in

Westminster were present during debates in the colonial assemblies, which generally allowed for unfettered reporting and discussion. Publications of pamphlets rose. Intermarriage between people of various national stocks gave rise to new generations who had no direct experience with Europe and believed themselves to be wholly American. Every aspect of life in the new nation, whose abundant natural resources could only be attained through steadfast efforts, fostered an entrepreneurial spirit that resented limitations.

The contest with France

Competing claims in North America

It was inevitable that France and Great Britain would compete for supremacy in North America. Without a ferocious struggle for dominance, the two powers could not coexist in the same region. This turned into one of the grand battles of modern history due to its century-long course and far-reaching effects. Between two peoples, two cultures, and two sets of governmental and religious institutions, there was a protracted battle. Its marches, sieges, and battles have a picturesqueness rarely seen in modern warfare since they were fought in the middle of a vast wilderness and involved Native American tribes on both sides. Louis de Buade, Comte de Palluau et de Frontenac, Antoine de la Mothe Cadillac, Louis-Joseph de Montcalm-Grozon, marquis de Montcalm, and James Wolfe, Jeffery Amherst, 1st Baron Amherst, John Forbes, and George Washington are just a few examples of the highly capable leaders it produced on the French side.

The French attempted to establish Canada as a colony in the first part of the 17th century but failed, despite Samuel de Champlain's leadership and the efforts of Jesuit, Recollect, and Franciscan clergymen. They failed to establish robust agricultural colonies while searching for fish, furs, and converts in a frigid, challenging area. Instead of encouraging self-government and individual initiative based on the English model, the despotic and paternal government in Paris tightly controlled the colonists. It also forbade anyone but Roman Catholics from emigrating rather than welcoming people of all faiths. Fewer than a thousand French settlers had made Canada their home by 1660. However, Louis XIV displayed a perceptive interest in New France when he ascended to the throne. His administration assisted missionaries and fur traders in spreading French culture throughout the Great Lakes region, sent out large numbers of emigrants, provided significant subsidies, and fostered exploration. The first bishop, François de

Montmorency Laval, was a capable, iron-willed man who arrived in Quebec in 1659 with a mission to establish the church as the dominating force in a bustling, active colony.

The greatest of the French rulers, the Count de Frontenac, rendered New France a real threat to English America in the last quarter of the nineteenth century. The remarkable voyages of Jacques Marquette, René-Robert Cavelier, Sieur de La Salle, and Louis Jolliet paved the path for the West during his reign, which spanned from 1672 to 1698 with one brief break. They explored a large portion of the upper Mississippi and Ohio valleys; La Salle travelled into Texas and descended the Mississippi to its mouth. Beyond Lake Superior, Médard Chouart des Groseilliers and Pierre-Esprit Radisson made their way into the land. Frontenac asserted the secular arm's dominance over the church with his customary skill and tenacity. The benevolent Huron and Erie tribes, where the Jesuits had gained the majority of their converts, had been all but wiped off by the hostile Iroquois. Frontenac reprimanded the Iroquois, momentarily weakening them. The English were frightened as New France grew. William and Mary replaced the Stuarts in Europe, who were subject to the French throne, in 1688, and William III, who had defended the Netherlands against Louis XIV's invasions, was prepared to resume hostilities. King William's War (1689–97) was the name given to the struggle as it quickly extended to North America.

Neither side made much progress in this initial phase of the protracted battle. The French ravaged the English colonies from Schenectady, New York, to Haverhill, Massachusetts, and along the coast of Maine, enlisting Indian allies in a brutal campaign. In exchange, the English planned an expedition that successfully overran Quebec and despatched a fleet of 34 ships under Sir William Phips to seize Port Royal in Acadia (now Annapolis Royal, Nova Scotia). The last Treaty of Rijswijk left everything just as it had been. Following a brief respite, the War of Spanish Succession in Europe (1701–14) was followed by Queen Anne's War (1702–13). While the first duke of Marlborough, John Churchill, achieved his magnificent successes in Europe, hostilities in America ended. The Anglo-American armies once more replied with descents on Canada after the French staged attacks with the Indians on exposed communities. Second England soldiers and British marines retook Port Royal when a new expedition towards Quebec once more failed, this time due to a shipwreck. The Treaty of Utrecht (1713), however, provided the British Empire with significant gains this time around, including Gibraltar and Minorca in Europe and Acadia, Newfoundland, and a sizable region of land surrounding Hudson Bay in America.

Not far away was the last strength test. The French constructed a belt of forts around British America as a precaution. They had founded New Orleans, Louisiana, in 1718, and Mobile, Alabama, in 1702. Nine significant installations served as the conduit between these Gulf ports and Quebec. Fort Chartres on the Mississippi opposite St. Louis, Missouri; Vincennes and French Fort on the Wabash River; Fort Miami on the Maumee River; Fort St. Joseph close to Lake Michigan's southernmost point; Michilimackinac and Sainte Marie on the upper lakes; Detroit, guarding Lake Huron; and Niagara, guarding Lake Erie. As a result, New France took control of the centre of the continent, relegating British America to the coast. The French held on to their crucial positions until King George's War (1744–48), the American phase of the War of the Austrian Succession (1740–48), erupted. To protect the mouth of the St. Lawrence River, they had erected a substantial stronghold at Louisbourg on Cape Breton Island, which also served as a haven for privateers who harassed New England trade. The New Englanders led by William Pepperrell mustered all their strength and stunned everyone by successfully conquering it. This was an amazing achievement. But after the war ended, Great Britain gave Louisbourg back to France.

The French acted once more to fortify their position. They constructed a new network of forts from what is now Erie, Pennsylvania (Presque-Isle) to the Allegheny River, laying claim to the whole Ohio Valley. Anglo-American land firms and fur traders had a keen interest in this area. When the French cautioned British commerce not to enter the nation, Virginia Governor Robert Dinwiddie sent George Washington to tell the French to do the same and to construct a fort in the location of modern-day Pittsburgh. Following this, the French took control of the area, built Fort Duquesne, and engaged in combat with Washington's Virginia militia. Thus began the two empires' last battle in North America.

The French and Indian War

In this bloody conflict, known in America as the French and Indian War (1754-63) and in Europe as the Seven Years' War (1756–63), the French had some advantages. With a stronger military and a larger population than Great Britain, France could conceivably send over more armed forces. In comparison to the loosely affiliated colonies governed by 13 independent administrations, New France's highly centralized government was better able to conduct war. A major advantage is the strategically located French forts.

However, the British colonies were certain of winning in the end. By 1754, they had a population of roughly 1,500,000, which was fifteen times greater than New France's. Operating from inside lines, they could attack at almost any point in the lengthy, sparsely populated French crescent extending from Louisbourg to New Orleans. This gave them a superior strategic position. The British fleet, which was more powerful than the French, could encircle the ports of New France and provide the army with better reinforcements and supplies. Finally, leadership was a strength shared by British America and Britain. James Wolfe, Jeffery Amherst, and William Howe were a trio of generals the French could not match, and such colonial officers as George Washington and Phineas Lyman demonstrated real ability. William Pitt the Elder, as prime minister of Great Britain, demonstrated himself to be a greater statesman than anyone in France.

The Anglo-American effort in the war initially fared poorly. In 1755, attacks on the French forts at Niagara and Crown Point on Lake Champlain were unsuccessful. An army led by Gen. Edward Braddock that was advancing to capture Fort Duquesne was ambushed and nearly decimated, losing its commander in the process. The marquis de Montcalm, a superb French soldier, came the following year and gave his army new life and structure. In 1757, he took Fort William Henry to the southernmost point of Lake George after immediately taking the British fortress at Oswego on Lake Ontario.

Later, he foiled a British effort to invade New France via Lake Champlain and Ticonderoga.

However, the stream shifted after Pitt dove headfirst into the tasks of war with zeal and insight. On a scale never previously seen in America, he mobilized the army and navy. He was able to enlist a higher level of cooperation from the colonial governments after they were finally moved by the seriousness of the conflict. With sufficient funding, competent generals, and unwavering will, a three-pronged war plan was pressed in 1758. The French had evacuated Fort Duquesne, which was taken by Gen. John Forbes. Amherst also captured the fortress of Louisbourg for the second and final time, and other troops took control of outposts on the Ohio River. The turning point in the American War occurred in the summer of 1759.

Following a futile two-month siege of Quebec, General Wolfe discovered a passage up the cliffs, led 4,500 soldiers up under cover of darkness, and on September 13 at daylight encountered Montcalm on the Plains of Abraham, dominating the city. Before death in battle, Wolfe was informed that the French were fleeing. During the rout, Montcalm was mortally wounded and carried back. The campaign, the war, and New France's future were all decided by the conquest of Quebec. The following year, Amherst defeated Montreal.

Except for two little fishing islands and the island of New Orleans, the Treaty of Paris (1763) transferred to Great Britain all French territories in America east of the Mississippi. Florida was given to Great Britain by Spain, which had joined the conflict. Ex forced New Orleans, which France ceded to Spain, and the whole eastern half of the continuo to join the British Empire. The fact that Louisiana and all French rights west of the Mississippi were given to Spain concerned Americans greatly and nearly immediately. Cuba and the Philippines were taken from the Spaniards by the British during the war; the fact that they were later covertly returned to Spain would later affect

American policy. The colonies' apparent freedom from the threat of assault appeared to be the greatest fact of all, though.

American social and cultural development

In 1754, seven of the colonies made an effort to develop a closer association plan. To negotiate a treaty with the Iroquois, their governors gathered in Albany. The contemporary Benjamin Franklin proposed a plan for the colonial union that, if approved, might have stopped or postponed the American Revolution. It demanded the creation of a congress with the authority to tax common goods, manage public resources, engage in negotiations with Indian tribes, and maintain armed troops.

Although the Albany Congress approved the plan, the colonies were too jealous of their independence to support it, and the British government was concerned that it may give the provinces an undue advantage. The 13 colonies were divided by geographic distance, travel challenges, disparities in temperament, religious beliefs, and customs, as well as provincialism of spirit. They exhibited poor cooperation even during the French-American war crisis.

However, the English language and its extensive literature, their shared exposure to representative systems of government, the English common law, and a fundamental commonality in viewpoint served to unite them. They all supported democracy in the sense of neral equality of opportunity and—following John Locke—the ownership of the fundamental rights to life, liberty, and property by every man. Barriers between the colonies gradually disappeared over the 18th century. Roads were made more accessible, coastal shipping grew, and intercolonial travel surged. There was widespread reading of a province's newspapers and pamphlets in neighbouring provinces. Young men who were immigrating freely included Alexander Hamilton from the British West Indies to New York and Benjamin Franklin from Boston to Philadelphia. Franklin served as postmaster from 1753 to 1755 while a post office was founded for British America. The lawyers and wealthy landowners of the various colonies shared similar ideologies; mechanic organizations were largely the same in Charleston, New York, or Boston.

Before the Revolution, there were seven separate colleges and a sizable number of private academies formed in the colonies. Yale was established in 1701, William and Mary in 1693, King's College (later Columbia) in 1754, and Harvard in 1636. The Great Awakening aided in the establishment of the colleges that would become Princeton (1746), Brown (1764), and Dartmouth (1800). (1769). AncAncientanguages, mathematics, logic, rhetoric, and astronomy were prioritized in college studies at first, but science subsequently gained ground. They gathered several sizable private libraries, with those of William Byrd in Virginia and Cotton Mather in Massachusetts being particularly notable.

Not all of the books were imported because American printers started producing 1,000 titles annually, mostly British. Franklin, who published essays, satires, academic articles, and collections of aphorisms, was the most varied American writer. Robert Beverley for Virginia, John Lawson for North Carolina, and Thomas Prince for New England all produced significant historical works in the first 60 years of the 18th century.

In the 60 years before the American Revolution, 13 colonists were elected to the Royal Society, including Cotton Mather of Massachusetts, Benjamin Franklin of Pennsylvania, and Alexander Garden of South Carolina. The synthesis of history, biography, theology, and science is knowknowhowMagnalia Christi Americana and unabated ably Mather's most significant piece of writing. In his essay Freedom of Will, Jonathan Edwards made a significant philosophical contribution (1754). The Pennsylvanian astronomer David Rittenhouse, the Harvard mathematician John Winthrop IV, and the botanist John Bartram all produced noteworthy work.

By 1750, every colony from Maine to South Carolina had numerous examples of extremely exquisite architecture, which was primarily English in design and detail. Excellent colonial artisans were trained by skilled cabinetmakers who immigrated from Europe. Benjamin West, who later became the director of the Royal Academy of Arts in London, John Singleton Copley, John Smibert, Robert Feke, and at least four other artists achieved such distinction that their work has been meticulously conserved and is highly valued. Philadelphia, Williamsburg, and Savannah all had excellent town planning.

By the end of the French and Indian War, the colonies had developed somewhat politically, economically, and culturally. Though they hardly felt inferior to their European peers, their lawyers, doctors, professors, and other professional men looked to Europe for standards. As communications improved, their intellectual ties to Great Britain grew stronger. British ideas, particularly those of Sir Edward Coke, the Commonwealthmen, and John Locke shaped political thought. Newspapers cut much of their foreign intelligence from British journals. Students pursued law at the London Inns of Court and medicine at the University of Edinburgh. Anglican priests had to be trained and ordained in England. In 1763, intercolonial ties were weak compared to the loyalty to the king and love for the motherland. Franklin believed that a union of the colonies was not feasible without Britain engaging in overt oppression.

The colonists, however, had no desire to take on a subordinate role within the empire after the French and Indian War. They were pleased with their warriors' track record in battle. They were well aware that Philadelphia was the second-largest city under British rule and that it was comparable to no other city outside of London in terms of being a centre for scholarship, scientific research, and the arts. They were aware that American business endeavours matched that of Britain and that, in some ways, they were advancing more quickly than any other people on the planet. The land was filled with an attitude of self-sufficiency. It was particularly prevalent among the mixed-blood settlers who had emigrated to the frontiers as well as among the artisans, mechanics, and labourers in the towns. When John Adams later said, "The Revolution was effected before the war began," he was speaking truthfully because the climate was shifting. People had the Revolution in their thoughts and their hearts.

The bid for independence (1763–83)

Early in 1763, King George III and his ministers declared the Seven Years' War to have successfully come to an end and began the difficult journey toward another conflict that would rock the British Empire to its very core. The secretary at war announced a ministerial plan to increase the British garrison forces in North America from a peacetime establishment of 3,100 men to 7,500 men in the House of Commons fifteen days after the Treaty of Paris was signed. He stated that these troops should "be supported the first year by England, thereafter by the Colonies." This straightforward suggestion sparked a debate that progressively pushed the American colonies toward independence.

Earlier disagreements

Before 1763, there had been some tension between Britain and the colonies; in fact, there had been so many disagreements that they could be considered chronic. Before the 17th century was over, the colonists in Connecticut and Rhode Island had succeeded in taking control of their local affairs after working hard to do so. They had run into opposition from proprietary and royal governors, council members, judges, and other officials in the various colonies. The elected lower house of the assembly was intended to be the dominating power across each colony. In these battles, the lower house had steadily taken control over legislative matters in general and money bills in particular. Additionally, it had encroached on the realm of executive power. Although in British theory the colonial legislatures were merely municipal bodies, it was claimed that in every colony the lower house was the equivalent of the British House of Commons for domestic affairs. In reality, this was the case. Of course, the Americans had not yet raised serious objections to the control the crown and Parliament exercised over American trade and manufacture, and neither had Parliament attempted to impose a tax on mainland colonists.

One could claim that Britain started its new colonial policy in 1759. British officials responded more forcefully to colonial issues in that year because the war's tide had significantly changed in favour of Britain (and its colonies). The Virginia Two-Penny Tobacco Act's rejection by the Privy Council in August 1759, London's growing insistence that directives to royal governors had legal force, orders from London requiring that new laws amending existing ones in Virginia, Massachusetts, and South Carolina should not go into effect until approved by the Privy Council, and demands from the imperial capital that judges in New York and New Jersey follow its laws are all indications of a significant change.

Between 1759 and 1763, the Anglican church provided additional complaints. Before the Seven Years' War, its agent, the Society for the Propagation of the Gospel in Foreign Parts, started "missions" in New England but then scaled back its operations. Following the guidance of Thomas Seeker, the archbishop of Canterbury, the Society established a new mission church in 1761 in Cambridge, Massachusetts, the epicentre of Congregationalism.

The archbishop wanted to stop the Congregationalists from sending missionaries to the Native Americans in addition to his proselytizing in Cambridge. Due to the influence of the archbishop, a 1762 Massachusetts Act intended to help them was rejected by the Privy Council the following year. The Congregationalists, who had long feared that the Church of England would send a bishop to America, were displeased by the Anglicans' activities, which were supported by British officials.

New colonial policy

Even though British colonial policy hadn't changed before the Seven Years' War, it did so shortly after. It is without a doubt significant that George III and the government led by John Stuart, the 3rd earl of Bute, sought to increase the garrison forces in North America. The British government reduced the regular army as the Seven Years' War concluded because it was expensive and because such a sizable force would not be required in peacetime.

The ministry's suggestion to keep 75 regiments in service, including 17 that would be stationed in North America, was accepted by Parliament. If it hadn't been made known that the colonists, especially those who lived in the West Indies, would be expected to pay their portion of the cost, Parliament might not have approved such an establishment, which was 50% greater than in 1754.

It seems unlikely that such a large number of soldiers were required to defend America; pbefore1754, when French Canada had posed a major threat, a far smaller army had been deemed enough. Garrison forces were required in the St. Lawrence Valley to quell a French Canadian uprising, and it made sense to station additional troops in East and West Florida to thwart any potential Spanish assault. Indian attacks were specifically targeted by other detachments that were to be kept in interior forts.

It is abundantly evident that the 13 colonies would only receive a small amount of the British army's direct attention in America and that the colonists would likely be required to pay a disproportionate share of the new organization's expenses. Even worse, neither the type of protection the colonies requested nor their willingness to contribute to its cost was questioned. It was more or less known in the past, at least by the colonies, that they had accepted parliamentary regulation of their industry and commerce only in exchange for protection, thus trouble would undoubtedly arise if the British government attempted to make the colonists pay.

Although the attempt to collect money from the colonists to pay for the new army in America was not expected to happen until 1764, the Bute ministry was prepared to act vehemently in colonial matters in the interim, and there was no slack when George Grenville became the first lord of the treasury and chancellor of the exchequer in April 1763 in a ministry formed by John Russell, 4th duke of Bedford. In just over two years in office, Grenville oversaw the implementation of a remarkable package of policies designed to fortify imperial defences, control colonial trade, and generate American money.

Proclamation line

The royal proclamation of October 7, 1763, which established the colonies of Quebec, East Florida, and West Florida as well as a sizable Indian reservation in the North American hinterland, was one of the Grenville measures. The wide region between the Appalachian Mountain crest and the Mississippi River was prohibited from settlement under the rules of the Proclamation of 1763. Additionally, because Native Americans were acknowledged as communal owners of the lands they occupied and because land purchases from them were made illegal unless done so at a public meeting presided over by a representative of the British government, occupation of large tracts of land east of the mountains was also restricted. The Proclamation of 1763's main goal was to stop, at least temporarily, imperial development westward because taking Indian territory was the main source of conflict with them.

Pontiac's insurrection (1763-64) inspired action in London. Whatever the justification, the limits constituted a new royal power play that constrained the influence of colonial assemblies as well as governors. Both the farmers who wanted to work the land and the speculators who wanted to buy land inexpensively despised the decree prohibiting the purchase and exploitation of Indian territories. The colonies, notably Virginia, protested vehemently; pioneers readily broke the proclamation, and speculators refused to let the crown crush their dreams of easy money. The policy, which was never completely implemented, gained favour with the Indians but also turned many farmers and several speculators—men of wealth and influence—against the mother country.

Trade with Native Americans

The Bedford-Grenville ministry would have attempted to control the trade between the colonists and the Native Americans if it weren't for the expense. Indian unrest was also a result of this trade, in which the Indians traded furs and deerskins for weapons, knives, mirrors, clothing, and rouge, mostly because the European dealers routinely defrauded their Native American customers. The trading was placed in the far-off Native American communities and hunting areas, making it impossible for colonial efforts to force the European traders to deal honestly. A "Plan for the Future Management of Indian Affairs" that would have placed rigorous limitations on the traders was completed by the London Board of Trade in July 1764. The "Plan" was never presented to Parliament since it would have cost a lot of money to carry out, hence commerce with the Indians continued unabated.

Regulation of maritime trade

However, it was conceivable to maintain tighter control over a much more significant aspect of the colonies' trade—their maritime traffic—without incurring additional costs. Once a British naval squadron arrived in Halifax, Nova Scotia, in April 1763, the commander was given orders to enforce the Navigation Acts to the best of his ability. The colonial governors also received similar directives. The American customs agency underwent renovations with the same goal in mind. That service had been understaffed, careless, and dishonest for a very long time. It had been spending up to £8,000 a year in fees while only receiving up to £2,000 a year in duties.

The customs agents were now directed to complete their work. As a result, by the end of 1763, the New England coast was subject to strict enforcement of the 17th-century Navigation Acts as well as the 1733 Molasses Act. The

Molasses Act imposed a sixpence per gallon levy on molasses imported from the foreign Caribbean islands to force the mainland colonists to purchase from the British West Indian islands. The duty was prohibitive and had it been collected, trade between the northern colonies and those subtropical isles would have ceased. However, it had not been. Importers now only have to pay a penny or a halfpenny per gallon thanks to the customs officers' initiative to lower the cost. But before the year was up in 1763, they started enforcing the Molasses Act exactly as the legislators in London had meant it, realizing that it was no longer prudent for them to change a law passed by Parliament. The colonies' marine trade was severely and further constrained as a result.

Grenville taxes of 1764

In the spring of 1764, Grenville persuaded Parliament to approve yet more measures to stifle American economic growth. He also imposed the first tax on the mainland colonies to raise funds to subsidize some of the costs of the troops who would be stationed there. Two of the many modifications made to the British business system in that year's revenue act were crucial. American protests had been received against the Molasses Act's implementation, along with a request that the tariff is reduced to one penny per gallon. The administration was warned that more than that would be too much for the traffic, but it chose not to heed the concerns.

The Bedford-Grenville government sought to safeguard the British West Indian planters from international competition, ensure tax income, or pursue both goals at once. The Sugar Act (1764), which imposed a threepenny charge on foreign molasses, as a result, stated explicitly in its preamble that its objective was to raise money for military expenses. The statute also authorized the establishment of an admiralty court to adjudicate cases involving individuals who disregarded trade regulations or failed to pay duties. For the merchants of the 13 colonies, Halifax would be a difficult location for this court to convene. The colonists had previously had access to juries in colonial tribunals, but in the new admiralty court, jurors would not be used. The colonial legislatures were prohibited from declaring their paper currencies legal tender by a new currency statute that was also passed by Parliament that spring. The colonies had partially printed money to fill their money shortfall, which was caused in part by a poor trade balance with Britain. Additionally, they had developed the habit of declaring it legal tender even though unity most frequently endangers the interests of both British and American creditors and disrupted the economy. Such legal tender legislation had been abolished by the British crown for New England in 1751; it was now prohibited throughout all the colonies as it appeared that Virginia and North Carolina would soon adopt such legislation.

The Stamp Act

The Stamp Act, which was enacted in the spring of 1765, is the most well-known and significant of all the Grenville legislation. The government estimated that the colonists should contribute roughly £200,000 a year, but the new molasses tax would only raise about £30,000 to help pay for the army. Grenville believed that stamp charges similar to those collected in Britain should be imposed on the colonies; such duties may take $75,000 or $100,000 out of the coffers of the colonies.

In the spring of 1764, Grenville declared that a stamped measure would be submitted the following year. He asserted that he would be open to considering an alternative that would accomplish the same thing, but he rejected the idea put up by representatives of numerous American colonies in London that the king requests the colonial legislatures to approve the necessary sums. One of them, Benjamin Franklin, naively suggested the creation of an American bank that would not only provide the British government with rich profits but also the colonies with a stable currency. In reality, Grenville was found to be in charge of the stamp duties. He got even more determined when complaints from America claimed they were both unlawful and overly burdensome, and the measure was submitted and swiftly passed as a result.

The Quartering Act

The Bedford-Grenville ministry pushed through significant changes to the yearly Mutiny Act in addition to the Stamp Act. One of them particularly expanded the statute to include America because some troops there had asserted—aided by certain civilians—that British officers had no legal standing east of the Atlantic. Desertion had been condoned and promoted by colonizers. Another amendment to the legislation mandated that colonial authorities provide British soldiers (commonly known as "Redcoats") stationed in cities and villages with food, drink, fuel, housing, and transportation at set prices. The colonists believed that this so-called Quartering Act (1765), as the stamp taxes, was unconstitutional even though there were few troops at the time in the American settlements and not much money would have been collected from them right away.

Conflicting views of the new policy

Britain had begun a new colonial policy as a result of the numerous actions made about the colonies by the Bute and Bedford-Grenville ministries as well as those of the years 1759–1763. The overall package of measures was spectacular and was largely new in fact if not in thought. There had come a major turning moment. The men who brought about the significant shift believed that Britain was only exerting its legitimate power and did not anticipate strong resistance from America. Franklin and other Americans in London believed that while the inventions would be despised across the seas, there wouldn't be any fierce opposition.

According to certain historians, the new British policy can be justified on constitutional as well as economic grounds. A compelling constitutional argument can be made for taxation without geographic representation when taking into account precedent in London, the Isle of Man, Jersey, Ireland, and common law. The economic case is less convincing. The argument goes that because the colonies were protected by the British army and navy and had low public debts and light taxes compared to Britain's high public debt and tax burden, the Americans were required to contribute to their fair portion of the cost. Overall, it is likely that American public financial responsibilities were lower than British ones.

However, this fact does not prove anything. To the prejudice of some colonial interests, particularly those of the tobacco growers in the Chesapeake Bay region, Parliament's channelling of American trade provided Britain with a sizable income. Furthermore, not all of the conflicts that led to the British debt and high taxes were started by the colonists, nor were they solely waged and funded by the British. A comparison of salaries is also a necessary component of any thorough discussion of economic issues. It seems unlikely that those of the Americans were greater than those of the British on a per capita basis. The claim that the abolition of sinecures and unearned pensions in Britain would have saved more money than the government would have made from taxing the colonists might also be made on behalf of the colonists.

The British innovations were viewed as tyranny by the Americans, who declared several of them to be unlawful. The term "tyrannical" may not entirely describe the new colonial strategy, but it is not wholly inappropriate either. They were prohibited from using the lands of the West for economic purposes, forced to pay for the protection of an enlarged army for which they had not asked, informed that maritime trade would be strictly regulated, and severely harmed by interference with their West Indian trade, at least mildly threatened by the Anglican church, suffered a significant loss in the medium of exchange, and were subjected to two very significant taxes for revenue imposed by a Parliament across the ocean in which they were not represented. All of these things caused them great harm They had also been warned that they may anticipate higher taxes. They could reasonably anticipate receiving more responsibilities if they submitted grudgingly.

The Stamp Act crisis

The colonists' uprising in 1765 followed one of the best British customs. They expressed their strong disapproval of the new molasses tax, the quartering of troops, the Stamp Act Congress that met in New York in October, and the admiralty courts with British judges and without American juries (though they later found nothing wrong with American admiralty courts without juries), among other things, through their provincial assemblies. They criticized the Stamp Act in particular for being burdensome and unconstitutional. They claimed that only themselves or representatives who would likewise pay the levy had the right to tax British subjects to raise money. Despite strong arguments to the contrary, this well-known notion was solidly based on English law and custom, as shown above. They caused the men who had been chosen to serve as stamp distributors to resign or refuse to do so by intimidation, mob violence, and threats of violence; stamps transported across the ocean were either destroyed or confiscated. Georgia saw the sale of a few. Otherwise, the colonists blatantly disobeyed Britain and demanded that the levy be repealed. Many of them stopped purchasing British goods to highlight their demand, and others failed to make payments to their British creditors.

It's possible that Britain and America would have fought soon had Grenville been in charge when word of the colonists' refusal to follow the Stamp Act reached London. The American defence of taxation without representation was completely rejected by him, and he was certain that the colonists could not be allowed to disrespect parliamentary authority. Unfortunately, he was pushed from office in July 1765, thus he had little control over the outcome.

A new cabinet, led by Charles Watson-Wentworth, 2nd marquess of Rockingham, and primarily made up of "Old Whigs," was more inclined to appease the colonists than to exert pressure. The Rockingham group did not contest Parliament's authority to impose the stamp taxes and did not want to give in to the demand for their repeal, but they found it simpler to do so because their political adversaries had brought about the unpleasant predicament they were in. William Pitt additionally pushed them to take steps toward an amicable settlement. He not only demanded the removal of the obligations, but he also vehemently agreed with the American position that they violated the Constitution. Pitt enjoyed enormous public respect even though he had few supporters in Parliament. Additionally, the American boycott's negative effects on British manufacturers and merchants—which were particularly felt during the postwar economic slump—suggested that they wanted it repealed. The "Old Whigs" and Rockingham decided to demand the repeal of the Stamp Act.

Repeal of the Stamp Act

The Rockinghamites did not give the colonists any constitutional concessions in their efforts to address the main American grievance. They claimed that the Americans should have obeyed parliamentary law and that, like the many opponents of the Stamp Act's repeal, they wanted the power of Parliament to be solemnly asserted in a public resolution. Despite Pitt's objections, the upshot was the Declaratory Act of March 1766, which declared that American Parliamentary authority was equal to that of British Parliamentary authority.

Along with repeal, the ministry demanded that the colonial assembly make up for property losses caused by mob action against Stamp Act supporters in the colonies. Additionally, the ministry was successful in getting the tax on molasses reduced in the Revenue Act of 1766 from threepence to one cent per gallon while also expanding it to include both British and foreign molasses.

Although the Americans found this movie to be financially advantageous, it should be noted that the revised tariff, which was levied on both British and foreign molasses, appeared very much like a levy for revenue. Thus, the Rockingham people agreed to forego the stamp fees and allow American trade with foreign islands in the West Indies, but they refused to make any other substantial concessions in either theory or practice.

However, Londoners were vehemently opposed to the abolition of the stamp tax. The ministry characterized the American constitutional position on taxation as narrowly as possible to appease the opponents of repeal. At least some American objections to the Bute-Bedford-Grenville strategy, most notably one from the lower chamber of the New York assembly, had denounced legislative taxation of any kind as unconstitutional. The ministry preferred to think that the colonists would be happy if the stamp duties were eliminated. Even if the Rockingham people made few compromises and tried their best to minimize the significance of those concessions, repeal would not have passed if George III had opposed it. The king instructed his followers who held positions related to the ministry that they had an obligation to support it out of respect; he told his other friends that they were free to pursue their preferences. The ministry won by a razor-thin margin as a result, and the Commons and the Lords reluctantly agreed.

The compromises were made unwillingly, and the objections of the Americans were far from totally allayed. However, the colonists mostly accepted them as a fundamental solution to the situation. They proudly renewed their commitment to Britain as they gleefully celebrated the repeal. Additionally, they excitedly started purchasing products from London, Bristol, and Liverpool merchants. They were delighted to leave the problem behind them so quickly and honourably. They remained silent about the ongoing complaints for a while. They would, of course, not be content with the situation as it stood in the spring of 1766, and as time went on, so would their perceptions of their rights within the empire.

To maintain a more or less lasting peace within the empire, further concessions from Britain would have been required. With enough time, the Rockingham people might have succeeded in establishing a fundamental conciliatory principle in British policy. When Pitt and George III ousted them from power and installed the ministry of "All the Talents" in July 1766, they did not give them the chance. Instead, they deprived them of it.

It is difficult to say if Britain and America would have reached a compromise if Pitt had continued to be in good health and held onto his position of power for a few more years after 1766. His reverence for the majesty of Britain and the cordial language he had grown accustomed to using toward the colonists do not prove that he would not have performed actions that were offensive to them. Certainly, the constitutional stance he had taken did not forbid actions that would be offensive to Americans. Pitt unintentionally helped to elect officials who shared Bute, Bedford, and Grenville's views on American thought. Historians have noted that compared to what is typically believed, they and their monarch were somewhat more tolerant of America. However, this new group of officials, which included Charles Townshend and the third earl of Hillsborough, gave the ministry of "All the Talents" the motivation for a second attempt to tax the colonists to raise money as well as for the deployment of the army for the the the repression in America. Pitt's friends never had genuine power over the government, even though Augustus Henry Fitzroy, the 3rd duke of Grafton, served as its leader until 1770. Their leader left the cabinet in 1768 because he was too ill to provide leadership.

The tasks of Townshend

Townshend, who pushed through Parliament in the spring of 1767 his infamous duties on tea, glass, lead, and papers, played a part in the Grafton ministry's zealous adoption of an American agenda. These import duties were openly stated to be imposed for monetary gain. Townshend thus resurrected a significant constitutional issue without having any realistic expectation of ever raising even a small portion of the money required to keep the American army in service. Additionally, rather than paying for military expenses, the initial earnings from the levies were to be used to support British authority in America by funding the salaries of British officials stationed there. Townshend was also in charge of the legislation that established the American Board of Customs Commissioners, which aggressively worked out of Boston beginning in November 1767.

By winning the passage of the Suspending Act in May 1767, which forbade the New York assembly from conducting any more work until it agreed with the Quartering Act's requirements, the Grafton ministry further enraged the colonists. In addition, Boston, Philadelphia, and Charleston each received a new admiralty court in 1768. The same ministry created a new western limit on American expansion in the spring of that year; this limit, which allowed settlement well beyond the Proclamation Line of 1763, was partly defined by the courses of the Ohio and Kanawha rivers.

A cabinet decision to relocate the American army was much more significant and was made at the same time. Gen. Thomas Gage, its supreme commander, had only ever used it once against the colonists before. He had instructed a force at Fort Pitt in 1765 to evict settlers who had made their homes beyond the Proclamation Line of 1763. Although he had dispatched 450 men into the settlements to provide a show of force if American resistance turned into insurrection, he had carefully avoided employing troops against the Stamp Act protestors. By 1768, it was dangerous to keep a significant contingent of British soldiers stationed in the colonies' urban centres. Although the

American army was reduced to 15 regiments to ensure economy and effectiveness, Gage was given the mandate to post "great bodies, in the provinces of Quebec, Nova Scotia, East Florida and in the middle colonies...to serve effectively upon any occasion whatsoever." As a result, Gage's force was concentrated along North America's eastern coast. Any emergency was defined as including a scenario in which British troops would be deployed against the colonists.

Colonial resistance

The Americans once more resisted these Parliamentary measures, which came to be known as the Townshend Acts, but less unanimously than during the Stamp Act troubles because many cautious colonists, especially men of property who had been alarmed by the rioting of 1765–166, were not in the mood to fight fiercely. The Americans had not previously made it plain that their objection to taxation without representation related to both the stamp tax and tariffs collected at their ports. They clarified their constitutional position under the guidance of John Dickinson, whose Letters from a Farmer in Pennsylvania to the Inhabitants of the British Colonies were widely published in colonial publications. Only obligations to regulate commerce were under Parliament's purview; both internal and foreign taxes for revenue were unlawful.

The Townshend tariffs' repeal was desired by the colonists. Additionally, they criticized the idea of using a portion of the revenue from the duties to pay the royal officials' salaries as a subversion of their long-standing form of government. The Americans were likewise dissatisfied with how congested their trade had become. After November 1767, American customs commissioners showed passion and vigour, as did the new admiralty courts after 1768. Due to the nearly complete enforcement of British shipping regulations, colonial ships and their cargoes were routinely impounded for minor infractions.

Several British officials were accused of plundering American merchants because they shared in the profits from these seizures. In some cases, this accusation was supported by evidence. The colonists once more used a boycott against British products to get the Townshend tariffs repealed. British manufacturers and merchants requested a repeal from Parliament as they had planned. To pressure British authorities and those colonies who backed them, the colonists once more used minor physical violence and the fear of it. The unpopular Boston customs commissioners requested military protection in the spring of 1768, alleging that they were seriously threatened. The ministry sent two more regiments from Ireland and instructed Gage to station two troops in the city.

In the summer of 1768, the British government was very active. In London, there was a lot of discussion about forcing the colonists to obey at the time and for several months following that. However, there was a lot of disagreement within the ministry. Townshend had passed away and could no longer insist that his debts be paid, and his successor, Lord Frederick North, was not a fan of severe measures. Gage was given the go-ahead to withdraw the troops from Boston in the spring of 1769, and it was declared that the Townshend's responsibilities would be much reduced. North proposed a measure eliminating all taxes except the one on tea on March 5, 1770. He claimed that the Townshend taxes should be eliminated since they harm trade. harm to he asserted that the tariff on tea had to be maintained to uphold Parliament's authority to impose external taxes to raise money and to end the Anglo-American crisis was resolved when Parliament gave in and made enough concessions.

The Boston Massacre

However, the day North introduced his repeal proposal, there was a troubling episode in Boston. Some of the troops dispatched into Boston were retained there until March 1770 because the royal governor, Thomas Hutchinson, requested that they be kept there. The Boston Massacre occurred on March 5 as a result of tension between soldiers and civilians. British soldiers were attacked by people who were throwing stones and chunks of ice at them, which resulted in the deaths of three Bostonians and the mortal wounding of two others. Due to the soldiers' bloodshed, the divide between Britain and America grew after a Boston jury found two of the men guilty of manslaughter.

The Gaspee

Before Rhode Islanders showed their opposition to royal decrees in June 1772, there were no other notable incidents. The Gaspee, a customs enforcement schooner, ran aground beneath Providence, Rhode Island, on June 9 while pursuing a smuggling vessel. In Narragansett Bay, illegal trade had grown significantly. That evening, the merchant John Brown led a group of men from Providence who boarded the Gaspee while it lay helpless and set it afire. When the ringleader's name could be established, rewards of £1000 were given, and Brown was taken into custody.

However, his release was brought about by the influence of his wealthy family, and a committee of investigation that met in Newport and Providence was unable to gather any solid proof. The British government was irritated by these legal lapses. The Americans were equally upset by reports that the lawbreakers would have been sent to Britain for trial if the commission had been successful.

The colonies join hands

Many individuals were angered when Massachusetts Governor Hutchinson later in the year stated that the home government would pay the salaries of the governors and justices of the superior court. The legislature was adamant about keeping such personnel in check, but it was unable to do so if Britain provided their salary. The Massachusetts towns supported Samuel Adams, James Otis, and others over the more traditional John Hancock. They served as an inspiration for the Boston town meeting, which established a Committee of Correspondence to correspond with other provinces and smaller towns.

As a result, a powerful engine was created. Similar committees were established by other provinces one at a time until their network connected the entire continent. Thomas Jefferson, Patrick Henry, and Richard Henry Lee were among the members of a standing committee for intercolonial exchanges that was established by the Virginia Burgesses as pioneers. Except for Pennsylvania and North Carolina, all of the colonies shared a web at the beginning of 1774.

The Boston Tea Party

Although the Townshend tax on tea irked most colonists, they opted not to argue about it. They consumed illicit Dutch tea as well as certain taxed British tea-based drinks. London, however, ought to have understood that no significant new action about the colonies should be done without careful study. American resistance to British legislation had occurred twice, and both times, Britain bowed. Britain would find it challenging to concede a third time. However, the Americans were put to the test once more. Following acting cautiously for several months as head of the government after 1770,

North pushed through his astonishing Tea Act of 1773. It changed the rules such that the East India Company could still outsell Dutch smugglers while paying the Townshend duty on tea. Additionally, the East India Company intended to restrict the sale of its tea to a select group of favoured colonial merchants, adding the problem of monopoly and aggravating American merchants who were not included in the selection. The colonists were generally determined to stop the selling of the tea when ships carrying it started to arrive in American harbours in the fall of 1773. If they allowed the Townshend duties to take thousands of pounds out of their pockets, wouldn't Parliament come up with more levies to impose on them? Nowhere in the colonies was the tea landed and sold. Boston responded vehemently. Boston residents dressed as Mohawk Indians held their Tea Party and threw 342 chests of tea into the harbour to ensure that it wouldn't be sold there. Later, similar gatherings were conducted in other ports.

The Intolerable Acts

The news that the colonists had once more disobeyed Parliament and damaged British property infuriated London. Boston was a hub for American resistance, so the North ministry set out to punish it and support British rule in Massachusetts. The king's advisors came up with the idea of punishing a city for the actions of its residents once they realized there was no way to pursue the disguised Tea Party members. The Boston Port Bill was the outcome, which prohibited access to the city's harbour beginning on June 1, 1774, unless it showed sufficient respect for British authority. The Massachusetts Government Act, which would have turned Massachusetts into a typical royal province and violated its charter of 1691, was later pushed through by the ministry to subdue Massachusetts.

Other acts contained new quartering arrangements and made it possible for a soldier or British official indicted for a crime while carrying out the major measures to change venue to another colony or Britain. These acts served to prepare for the troops that would be sent into the colony to maintain order. General Gage was chosen as the colony's governor, given the go-ahead to enforce the harsh laws, and given the go-ahead to post troops in Boston to intimidate its citizens. These actions, which Americans have variously referred to as the Coercive Acts or the Intolerable Acts, were to serve as a warning to the other colonies.

The Quebec Act, which was passed at the same time as the other acts, was not related to them, but the colonists grouped it in with them. Because it established an authoritarian government for Quebec and reaffirmed the church's rights, it worried the colonists. Additionally, it stretched Quebec's borders to the Ohio River.

Massachusetts revolted as Boston refused to pay for their Tea Party. The lower chamber of the government demanded a Continental Congress and refused to pay for the Tea Party. In the summer of 1774, when Gage attempted to form a new royal council, those who were outside of Boston were forced to quit. A few were incarcerated. Except for the city and its surroundings, where Gage was preparing for armed confrontation, royal authority vanished. The Massachusetts men were prepared to fight rather than submit by the beginning of September. Gage had already started defending Boston from potential attacks, but he lacked the strength to move against the colonists. He kept bringing in warriors until the majority of his army was assembled in Boston.

The lower house in Massachusetts was also preparing for war at the time. It seized control of the province outside of Boston in October 1774. It transformed into a revolutionary administration by putting on the mask of a provincial congress. In a letter to his superiors in London, Gage advised them to send numerous reinforcements if they decided to employ the army to crush resistance since all of New England would fight fiercely. In addition, he added, there was a good chance that the other colonists would aid the people of New England.

As an alternative, he suggested that Britain impose a naval blockade to quell the rebellious spirit in the colonies. Making concessions, as had been done in 1766 and 1770, was a third option that he opposed. He was very clear that Britain needed to make a wise choice.

In the fall of 1774 and the winter that followed, London received reports from the other colonies that were not very upbeat. As conflict became more likely, more colonies decided to support Britain, joining the tiny minority who had previously supported the mother country. However, because they were a minority and could do nothing to control individuals who disagreed with British policies, they were referred to as patriots. The First Continental Congress, which convened in Philadelphia in the fall of 1774, was attended by delegates from every state that had followed Massachusetts' lead in converting their lower houses of parliament into revolutionary bodies, setting up committees of safety, dealing harshly with aggressive loyalists, and sending protests to London.

Revolution and independence

The First Continental Congress

The patriot cause gained more depth, vigour, and breadth as a result of the First Continental Congress. Its 56 members, who represented all of the colonies except Georgia, were respectable and responsible men who worked as lawyers, country gentlemen, and merchants. America followed them. They made it obvious that the other colonies would not stand by and let Britain conquer Massachusetts. They called the Quebec Act and the Intolerable Acts, as well as several other actions enacted after 1764, unconstitutional and demanded their repeal. They want a return to the 1763 "good old days."

However, they desired more than that. They encouraged the monarch to give up the power to choose the council members in the royal colonies. They challenged the legitimacy of Parliament far more openly than the Stamp Act Congress did, but they were very careful not to ask it for relief.

However, Congress did send a letter to the British people and an appeal to the monarch. It also supported a declaration of rights that charged the British administration with breaking the rights guaranteed by the colonial charter, the rights of British subjects, and the basic human rights importance of including natural rights cannot be overstated.

Although some of their leaders had already cited the rights of humanity, the colonists had previously opted to rely primarily on the rights of British subjects. The protection of American liberty by English law and custom had not proven to be unbreakable fortresses. The Americans were shifting their focus from the more specialized debate over the rights of British subjects to the more fundamental discussion of a person's natural rights.

Congress made an exceptional choice. It created what it termed the Association, again pleading with Britain to repent and repeal. Defenders of American liberty were urged to band together to prevent the importation or consumption of goods from Britain or the British West Indies after December 1, 1774, and to halt the exportation of colonial goods, except rice, to the same locations after September 10, 1775, if Britain refused to budge. Since the Congress' wishes were upheld everywhere, 13 colonies organized a systematic boycott of British products, which was a stunning spectacle. The delegates left in October 1774 with plans to meet again in May 1775 to conduct any additional actions that might be required. The patriots started preparing for battle in the winter.

Parliament's response

Pitt, Edmund Burke, and John Wilkes pushed for rapprochement with America in Parliament at the beginning of 1775. The opposition sternly warned against using force to try to solve the issue. The colonists would fight, according to its speakers, who also expressed concern that France and Spain would embrace the chance of an Anglo-American conflict to recoup the losses they had sustained in the Seven Years' War. Due to the effects of the American boycott, British manufacturers and traders also pushed for an effort to win over the Americans. However, George III and his political supporters controlled the outcome because they had twice as many votes in Parliament as their rivals.

The king had stated his belief that Britain ought to assert its sovereignty as early as November 1774. Most of his advisors agreed with him and were even eager to resort to violence. Because they both regarded the Americans and the opposition as enemies of the ministry, they laughed off their arguments. They sprang into action with the monarch's backing and the support of a sizable portion of the populace.

The king and his ministry decided against Gage's advice and that of other knowledgeable military men in Britain. They also overcame Lord North's resistance and that of his stepbrother William Legge, 2nd earl of Dartmouth, who had been appointed colonial secretary in 1772. The secretary of war, Lord William Barrington, voiced great doubt that Britain could send enough soldiers into battle to conquer the colonies and recommended a naval blockade as a more effective form of coercion. Dartmouth and North wanted to keep things peaceful.

In the end, they were powerless to resist the will of their allies, but the prime minister stressed that no use of the army should be made without first making an effort to settle. Both economic and military coercion received backing from Parliament.

As a result, after being persuaded to use force three times, Britain ultimately entered a war. Reluctantly, Parliament agreed to Lord North's conciliation resolution, which said that it would no longer tax any colonies that contributed their due part of the monies required for imperial defence through their assemblies. Each colony received it separately, which the colonists inexorably perceived as an attempt to foment separation among them. The Continental Congress did not receive any communication. One was dispatched to Gage, who was instructed to employ his troops to the fullest extent possible.

The decision for independence

The Second Continental Congress proclaimed American independence fifteen months after hostilities started. Before 1775, most patriots wanted to stay within the British Empire. The bulk of them began to believe that their happiness was better guaranteed outside the empire as the battle dragged on. They were compelled to seek a complete break due to several factors, including the bloodshed by British troops, attacks by the British navy on American ships, sailors, and ports, the enlistment of African Americans, Native Americans, and German (Hessian) mercenary troops by Britain, the patriots' growing conviction that Britain would not accept an accommodation, and the conviction that if an agreement with Britain were reached, it would lead to the end of the United States. Reluctantly and hesitantly, they took steps toward declaring their independence. They had an emotional bond with Britain, were aware of the safety the imperial connection had provided, were concerned that foreign help may result in foreign dominance, and many of them were worried that independence would result in economic and social equality.

Once independent, they must establish a solid republican administration along the Atlantic coast for a region that stretches over a thousand kilometres. Was it possible?

Many of the patriots were still holding out hope that Britain would provide reasonable peace terms months after the shooting started. They hoped that the brothers Adm. Richard Howe and Gen. William Howe, who was chosen as peace commissioners in 1776, would bring with them solid foundations for a settlement. The majority of the patriots stayed up, nevertheless, when it became clear that Britain relied heavily on military might. It had an impact that the colonies had been proclaimed to be in a state of rebellion in August

1775, and it had a significant effect that the Prohibitory Act, which removed the king's protection from the colonies and placed them under naval blockade, had been passed in November 1775. The sane George Washington had concluded by January 1776 that he would be content with nothing less than separation. The Second Continental Congress, representing all of America, finally severed the last link between the colony states and Britain on July 2, 1776, stating that "These United Colonies are, and of right ought to be, free and independent states." Two days later, it ratified the Declaration of Independence, which outlined the justifications for the patriots' actions.

The natural rights of people and the law of contracts were the only arguments the patriots used to support their position in the Declaration of Independence. Thomas Jefferson and Congress demonstrated to their satisfaction that George III had blatantly breached the contract and invoked the right of revolution, disregarding Parliament as a "pretended" assembly.

Howe's peace mission

On the same day that the Congress proclaimed independence, General Howe arrived at Staten Island. Until the uprising was put down, he and his brother were not allowed to communicate with the patriots other than to grant forgiveness to those who would lay down their arms. However, they were able to offer some extremely intriguing terms following the defeat of the resistance. They may pardon all rebels, reinstate royal protection, and demand that Rhode Island and Connecticut be transformed into royal colonies, or at the very least that the appointment of their governors is subject to royal approval. There were no American concessions made here.

However, the commissioners were also allowed to offer a financial proposal. The core of it stemmed from Lord North's accommodative resolution, which stated that if the colonies (except Georgia, which was not to be asked to pay anything) agreed to contribute 10%, even 5%, of the cost of maintaining the imperial army, navy, and ordnance, they would be exempt from Parliament's regressive taxation.

Many supporters of American rights may have found the deal to be alluring before the conflict. Since the Patriots weren't forced into surrender, it wasn't even presented to them as it was. These recommendations suggest an effort to try and appease the colonists following the end of hostilities, assuming there was no governmental attempt to deceive. The Patriots were left to speculate about what would happen to them if they were beaten because they were unaware of the stipulations. It was a stunning failure of British propaganda that the terms were not made public. There was a military failure.

Early in 1775, during parliamentary debates, John Montagu, 4th earl of Sandwich, the first lord of the admiralty, said that the British army could easily defeat the colonists. History has shown that Lord Barrington's proposal to rely primarily on a naval blockade, which was rejected by his superiors, was sound advice because it would have cost Britain less in terms of lives and resources to lose the war if it had done so. Barrington's scheme might not have succeeded, but that is far from definite either. The colonies might not have sought independence if there had been a blockade that severely damaged the American economy without endangering American lives, and it might have instead resulted in an Anglo-American agreement. In any case, there would have been revenue from the looted American ships and cargoes, as well as financial savings from just having the army as a backup. Nevertheless, the ministry supported Sandwich's plan, attempted to annex the colonies, fell short of its objective, and eventually was forced to admit defeat.

Britain did not give up all of its prospects for victory by using methods revered by tradition to put down the uprising. Even in the type of war, it fought after 1775, Britain had significant advantages. About four times as many people lived there as in the American colonies. Additionally, only about half of Americans were ardent patriots, with the other half either neutral or supporting the British government.

However, until France interfered, there was little excitement for the war in Britain. Britain had a navy that the patriots could never hope to match, a well-established administration, the ability to produce all required military hardware, significant economic wealth, and access to both currency and credit. The knowledge of its army and naval leaders and the presence of thousands of veterans who had battled on land and at sea were additional sources of power. However, even though hundreds of supporters had rallied behind the British flag, the patriots were able to send more soldiers into the field of battle than Britain.

The Americans were outnumbered in just a handful of the war's conflicts. Additionally, the patriots could deploy ships and sailors to sea to deal serious blows to the British merchant navy, and they did so. They possessed enough material wealth to last through a protracted conflict, but they struggled to put that wealth to military use due to a lack of American cash and credit.

Geographical factors heavily favoured the Americans because of the 3,000 miles (4,800 km) of water that separated them from the British Isles, which created a significant supply problem for the British and slowed and uncertain communication between British field officers and their superiors in London. The overwhelming majority of colony states worked against British victory. The fact that the Americans' ability to resist would not be significantly harmed by the loss of numerous of their cities was another crucial advantage. America resembled a serpent without any vital organs in both shape and substance.

The ability of the patriots to retreat into the interior and strengthen themselves as they did so gave them a distinct advantage over the British forces, who were forced to maintain bases and supply lines while they pursued. Several significant battles in the interior would end in British army defeat. Furthermore, keeping the field until Britain became sick of the war was all that was required of the Americans, not destroying the British forces. Additionally, the patriots were familiar with their own country, and many of them were deeply devoted to their cause.

The turning point

Gen. John Burgoyne's signature of the Convention of Saratoga in October 1777 and the ensuing French government decision to form an alliance with the Americans in February 1778 marked the turning point of the war from a military and diplomatic perspective. France and Spain joining the conflict as adversaries brought new and difficult duties upon Britain. Burgoyne's defeat and France's impending entry into the fight alarmed London, which prompted the Carlisle Commission to be sent to grant the Americans autonomy inside the empire, a plan that the Congress rejected. Additionally, it made the British army and fleet in America spend the majority of 1778 on defence.

When a French navy led by Charles Hector, Comte d'Estaing crossed the Atlantic and momentarily denied Britain easy control of North American waters, the shape of things to come loomed. The French admiral, however, was ineffective. Admiral Richard Howe and Gen. Sir Henry Clinton, who had taken over for William Howe, immediately carried out an order to evacuate Philadelphia before d'Estaing's arrival. Lord Howe joined Clinton in New York after he successfully crossed New Jersey with the majority of the army, repulsed Washington's onslaught at the Battle of Monmouth, and arrived there in safety. Plans were made by Washington and d'Estaing for land and marine assault on New York, but they were never carried out.

Additionally, they were stopped from launching a coordinated attack on Newport. To the West Indies, the French fleet set off. When d'Estaing returned to North American waters in 1779, he took part in a Franco-American attack on Savannah that a British force bloodily repelled. A French squadron with a small French army established itself in Newport in 1780 after the British had left. Clinton was deeply concerned by the prospect of the French navy gaining control, however momentarily, of American seas and collaborating successfully with the patriots.

Clinton, who had occasionally shown intelligence and sass as a subordinate, was cautious as the commander in chief because of the French threat. Attacking Washington, who hung around New York from 1778 to 1781, he hardly did more than making a gesture. Except for the deep south, Clinton engaged in an endurance campaign, to which he added significant raids in Connecticut and Virginia as well as attempts to attract American political figures. It is difficult to predict what would have happened in the end if such a policy had been implemented consistently and systematically. By 1780, the Continental money had lost all of its value, making it impossible for Congress to pay its men on time. Requisitioning supplies from the states was necessary. The British also experienced financial difficulty, so it's far from likely that they would have outlasted the patriots in an endurance war. The outcome would have been the same even if the conflict had ended less abruptly and tragically.

War in the south

Clinton did not insist that his cautious approach be implemented in the southern states, as it turned out. Because there were many loyalists in the Carolinas and Georgia and the patriot forces there were weak, he allowed Lord Cornwallis to engage in aggressive exploits there. A British expedition led by Clinton conquered Savannah at the end of 1778, and it became clear to Clinton that greater British forces might reach Charleston. A force led by General Clinton encircled the city in the spring of 1780 and forced its surrender with more than 5,000 American soldiers.

When it fell, South Carolina's and Georgia's patriots were shocked, and their resistance briefly crumbled. Clinton built garrisons at a number of the forts in their interior after being encouraged to increase activities. Forced to leave Cornwallis in charge in the deep south, he told him to defend the new gains and not to engage in any costly endeavours that may risk the British control of South Carolina and Georgia. Additionally, he told Cornwallis that, should the time come, he would be able to lead British raiding units in Virginia.

The British army in the deep south would have been primarily focused on maintaining the advances previously gained had Clinton stayed there, but Cornwallis was made of different stuff. He was fearless and brash, more of a warrior than a thinker.

The British hold over South Carolina and Georgia was soon in jeopardy, and the two states' patriots resorted to partisan fighting as bigger patriot troops moved toward them from the north. In August 1780, Cornwallis defeated an American army led by Gen. Horatio Gates at Camden, South Carolina, while it was leaving North Carolina. He decided to invade North Carolina's interior after his straightforward victory. He had to retreat after a force of 1,000 loyalists that had advanced alongside him were surrounded and killed at the Battle of King's Mountain that autumn.

Then, by the letter, if not the spirit, of his orders, he might have prudently remained on the defensive. He drove into the interior of North Carolina a second time after obtaining reinforcements. He continued after Gen. Daniel Morgan routed a British detachment of over a thousand men led by Col. Banastre Tarleton at Cowpens in January 1781.

Morgan joined Gen. Nathanael Greene, who had taken over leadership of the Continental troops in the South, while Cornwallis continued to aggressively pursue Greene. Even though his force was deteriorating due to hardship and disease, he pursued Greene to the Virginia border. Greene, now backed up, followed him when he eventually turned around. At Guilford Courthouse in March, Cornwallis attacked Greene with 4,500 men but was ultimately driven back by just 1,900 men, less than half the number of soldiers he had started with. Cornwallis was unable to remain in North Carolina's interior, though. He had to retreat and protect the British victories in South Carolina and Georgia, as was required by caution and his orders, which were very clear. He left the duty of guarding the British victories in the deep south to his subordinates and instead marched the remnants of his army to the coast of North Carolina and then to Virginia to embark on a new adventure.

Yorktown

Cornwallis ran into trouble in Virginia. He gathered an army of 7,000 soldiers by adding British raiding contingents there to the men he led from North Carolina, waged a hard campaign against the rebels without achieving a definitive victory, and then established a base at Yorktown. Clinton advised him to lead the remaining soldiers north while leaving some of his men to guard the base. Clinton gave Cornwallis the freedom to use his entire force to defend Yorktown as he saw fit.

Then both land and sea quickly encircled Cornwallis. From the West Indies, a strong French fleet led by Admiral François-Joseph-Paul, Comte de Grasse, arrived in the Chesapeake. The British fleet at New York was outclassed by this one.De Grasse was able to push the New York fleet away from the opening of the harbour because George Rodney, commanding in the West Indies, was unable to send enough ships after him to restore the balance. He was joined by the French squadron at Newport. Along with several thousand other colonists, Washington went swiftly south with the French soldiers from Newport. He had 17,000 men to block Cornwallis' land retreat and lay siege to Yorktown with these.

The outer fortifications of Yorktown were breached by Franco-American assaults. From New York, a British rescue mission was dispatched, but it was too late and presumably too feeble to save Cornwallis. On October 19, 1781, he gave up.

The British acknowledged Yorktown as being pivotal. Aggression on the coast had resulted in defeat, while aggression in the interior of the United States had resulted in significant losses and few benefits. Would the result have been different if the French fleet hadn't shown up? Before the French arrived, the brash Cornwallis was not making any progress. Thankfully, his enthusiasm accelerated the American end of the conflict.

The Treaty of Paris

The preliminary Anglo-American peace settlement of 1782, which was a part of the Treaty of Paris in 1783, reflected the military verdict in North America. The American commissioners were Henry Laurens, John Jay, John Adams, and Benjamin Franklin. By its provisions, Britain acknowledged the United States' independence (and the end of the American colonies) by giving the countrywide borders, including the Mississippi River on the west. Although Spain received East and West Florida, Britain kept Canada.

The settlement of American private obligations owed to the British people, American access to the Newfoundland fishery, and a recommendation by Congress to the states in favour of treating the loyalists fairly all had provisions added.

The majority of the supporters remained in the new nation. Up to 37,000 Tories might have immigrated to Canada, whereas fewer went to Britain or the British West Indies. Many of them had been expelled by American states after serving as British soldiers. After a generation, the less fervent and more cautious Tories who remained in the United States viewed the break with Britain as final and could no longer be distinguished from the patriots.

The American nations regarded the loyalists brutally both during the war and immediately after as dangerous foes. They were constantly penalized, frequently denied their property, and frequently denied their civil rights. Those who stood out were typically exiled under the penalty of death. Roughly 2,300 loyalists received compensation from the British government for property losses, totalling about £3,300,000. Additionally, it provided posts, pensions, and land concessions to loyalists so they could reconstitute themselves.

Quick questions

The American Revolution: What was it?
What sparked the American Revolution?
What significant factors gave rise to the American Revolution?
During the American Revolution, which nations supported the colonies?
The American Revolution was a civil war in what way?